Art in the Nineteenth Century

JILLIAN POWELL

Wayland

ART AND ARTISTS

Ancient Art
Art in the Nineteenth Century
Impressionism
Modern Art
Renaissance Art
Western Art 1600-1800

Cover *The Awakening Conscience* by William Holman Hunt. (Tate Gallery, London.)

Title page *The Gleaners* by Jean-François Millet. (Musée d'Orsay, Paris.)

Series and book editor: Rosemary Ashley
Designer: Simon Borrough

First published in 1994 by
Wayland (Publishers) Limited
61 Western Road
Hove
East Sussex, BN3 1JD, England

© Copyright 1994
Wayland (Publishers) Limited

British Library Cataloguing in Publication Data
Powell, Jillian
    Art in the Nineteenth Century. – (Art & Artists Series)
    I. Title   II. Series
    709.032

ISBN 0-7502-0976-3

Typeset by Dorchester Typesetting Group Limited
Printed and bound by L.E.G.O. S.p.A., Vicenza, Italy

The publishers would like to point out that where there are variations in spelling or definition regarding the artists and works in this book, the example of the *The Penguin Dictionary of Art and Artists,* reprinted in 1991, has been followed.

Picture Acknowledgements
The photographs in this book were supplied by: Archiv für Kunst und Geschichte 7, 12, 13 (left), 14, 15, 16, 18, 22, 26, 37, 41; Bridgeman Art Library main cover picture, ii, 4, 5, 8, 9 (left), 10, 13 (right), 17, 19 (both), 21, 23 (both), 24 (both), 25, 27 (both), 28, 29 (right), 30, 31, 32, 33, 34, 35, 38, 42 (both), 43, 44, 45, 46 (both); Christies Colour Library 29 (left); Hulton Deutsch Picture Library 9 (right), 11, 39 (right); Visual Arts Library cover, 20, 35, 39 (left); Wayland Picture Library/Tate Gallery 6-7,/British Museum 36, 40.

CONTENTS

1 INTRODUCTION

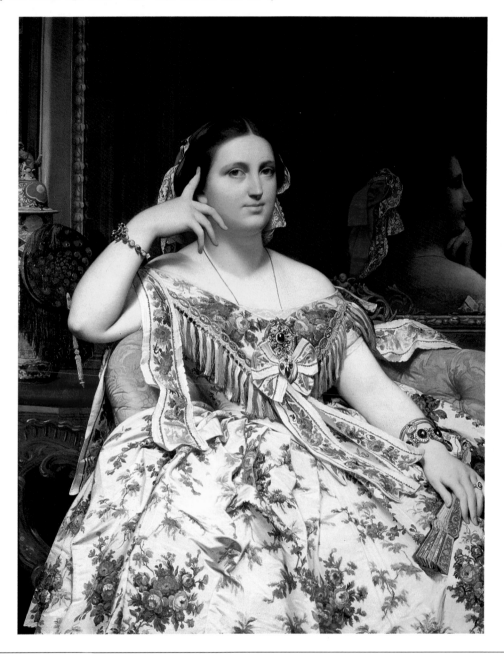

The nineteenth century was an age of change, introducing the modern world. Wars and revolutions brought social and political change to Europe and America. Industrialization changed people's lives and the environment in which they lived and worked. Railways and steam ships allowed faster travel and expanded overseas trade, while telephone and telegraphic systems opened up communications. The United States took on a new importance in international affairs and European countries enlarged their empires through colonization.

Industrial growth gave wealth and power to the manufacturing and trading middle classes.

Left In his *Portrait of Madame Moitessier*, the French painter Jean Auguste Ingres has shown her in splendid dress and jewellery, seated in a luxurious drawing room. Her pose, borrowed from Classical art, gives her the grandeur of a goddess. (National Gallery, London.)

Above In the nineteenth century, landscape became an ever more popular subject for painters in Europe and North America. Nature provided an escape from modern industrial life and paintings such as *Twilight in the Wilderness*, by the American artist Frederick Edwin Church, could inspire a sense of wonder and spirituality. (Cleveland Museum of Art, Ohio.)

They began to take a new interest in their homes and in public buildings such as town halls, factories, warehouses and railway stations. There was a steady demand for new buildings, and for sculpture and paintings to decorate them. In earlier times, artists had relied on the Church or the State for patronage. Now, they had to compete for patrons by exhibiting their works in public exhibitions and galleries.

Architects, also, entered their designs for buildings in public competitions. This inspired a variety of new styles; Neoclassicism, Romanticism, Realism and Impressionism all developed in the nineteenth century.

Derby Day by the English painter William Frith. Frith used the modern art of photography to provide many of the details for his panoramic view of the famous race meeting. (Tate Gallery, London.)

While the Industrial Revolution brought wealth to some, there was a growing awareness throughout the century of social discontent and poverty, especially in the crowded cities of Europe and North America. Nineteenth-century art and literature often reflected a desire to escape from the modern age, whether in nature, in a romanticised past – usually the Middle Ages – or in faraway places like North Africa.

The attraction of life and art of the Middle Ages reflected a longing for the certainties of a lost age of faith. In 1859, Charles Darwin's *On the Origin of Species* challenged the story of the

Beata Beatrix by the Pre-Raphaelite artist Dante Gabriel Rossetti. He painted this picture as a memorial to his wife Elizabeth Siddal, who died in 1862. The painting represents the death of Beatrice, loved by the thirteenth-century Italian writer Dante. It shows a bird, messenger of death, dropping the poppy of sleep into Beatrice's hands. (Tate Gallery, London.)

Creation as told in the Bible, undermining religious faith and bringing a new mood of doubt and uncertainty. Artists were also facing new challenges, such as the art of photography, which meant that now it was possible to record accurate images, thus questioning the very nature of the artist's role.

Photography, and cheaper methods of printing such as wood engraving and lithography, made reproductions of artists' works available to a much wider audience. These new media also spread knowledge of foreign countries, archaeological discoveries and the art of previous centuries, encouraging an interest in

The Winnowers by the French Realist artist Gustave Courbet. He was one of the first artists to take an interest in painting the lives of ordinary working people. (Musée des Beaux-Arts, Nantes.)

artistic styles of the past. Artists responded to the challenge of photography in different ways. The Pre-Raphaelites in England, the French painter Eugène Delacroix and the American artist Thomas Eakins, all used photographs to help them with their painting. The Victorian artist William Frith (1819–1909), popular as a 'genre' artist (painting everyday activities), used several photographs of the grandstand crowds on Derby Day to compose his famous scene at the races (see previous page). Some painters tried to make their paintings look like photographs, using minutely-detailed brushwork and a smooth finish. Others reacted against the photographic image, believing the artist should create his or her own image. Free brushwork, swirling paint and the dominance of colour, tone and pattern over line meant that by the end of the century the Impressionists and artists like James Abbot McNeill Whistler (see also pages 44-5) and Philip Wilson Steer were heralding a new age of abstract art.

The interior of Joseph Paxton's Crystal Palace. It was opened in London's Hyde Park by Queen Victoria for the Great Exhibition in 1851.

Arrangement in Gray and Black, better known as *The Artist's Mother,* by James Abbot McNeill Whistler. Whistler's streamlined composition and strong sense of shape and pattern anticipate art of the following century. (Musée d'Orsay, Paris.)

In architecture, the mass production of new materials such as cast iron and steel, and the demand for different kinds of building, brought new possibilities for architects and engineers. Iron and steel were used to span the vast spaces needed for exhibition halls and railway stations.

The Crystal Palace, built entirely from cast iron and glass in London's Hyde Park, was designed by Sir Joseph Paxton to house the Great Exhibition of 1851. The Eiffel Tower, in Paris, was constructed in steel by Gustave Eiffel, in 1889. Lack of space in cities, new materials, and the invention of the lift, encouraged high-rise building. As a result the first sky-scrapers were built in New York and Chicago by the end of the century. Historical styles of architecture (known as 'Revivalist') were widely used for every kind of building: from grand Neoclassical museums and town halls to soaring Gothic Revival churches.

2 NEOCLASSICISM AND ROMANTICISM

This *Portrait of Madame Recamier* by Jacques Louis David, is a perfect example of Neoclassical simplicity. (Musée du Louvre, Paris.)

During the eighteenth century, archaeological discoveries in Greece and Rome and a revival in the study of Classical art and literature, encouraged the development of a new artistic style: Neoclassicism. In France, the Neoclassical style became very fashionable during the French Revolution (1789-99), when heroic, moral themes from Classical history were chosen to inspire the revolutionary cause. The Neoclassical style is best represented by the works of the painter Jacques Louis David (1748-1825) and the sculptors Antonio Canova and Bertel Thorvaldsen (see chapter 6).

David's *Oath of the Horatii*, painted in 1785, illustrated the Neoclassical ideals of a serious, moral theme, through a simple composition with cool, plain, colours. Sculptors, too, chose Classical subjects, carving statues in calm poses inspired by Greek or Roman sculpture, in

The Battle of the Styles
After the Houses of Parliament in London burned down in 1834, a competition was held to choose the design for the new building. Neoclassical designs competed with Gothic Revival design in a grand 'Battle of the Styles'. In the end, the Gothic Revival design won and Sir Charles Barry (1795-1860) was appointed architect, with Augustus Pugin (1812-52) responsible for the design of the detail and furnishings.

white Carrara marble which was polished to a smooth finish.

By the early nineteenth century, the fashion for Neoclassicism was influencing architecture, furniture, ceramics, textiles and clothing. Even hairstyles 'in the Greek fashion' became popular. Artists continued to look to Classical history and mythology for themes, but they also applied the Neoclassical style to subjects taken from the Bible and from poetry. Jean Auguste Ingres (1780-1867) who was a pupil of David, painted portraits and nudes in the Neoclassical style as well as historical and literary subjects. Ingres believed that line was much more important than colour in a painting, and whatever their subject, his paintings have a quality of stillness and calm derived from the works of Classical Greece and Rome (see page 5).

Soon, a different mood was influencing literature and the visual arts. Neoclassicism was being challenged by new interests: the exotic and the faraway, the distant past (especially the romanticised Middle Ages), and the new importance attached to feelings and emotions. The calm, order and sense of purpose which were features of the Neoclassical style were replaced by the drama, struggle and emotion of Romanticism.

Artists in Europe and America began to explore new subjects. In France, Romanticism reflected the mood of melancholy and despair which followed defeat at the Battle of Waterloo in 1815, at the end of the Napoleonic Wars. Artists painted soldiers fleeing the battlefield, horses rearing in terror and scenes of fear and destruction.

For his *Raft of the Medusa* Théodore Géricault (1791-1824) took a tragic and scandalous subject from the news. The *Medusa* was a government-owned ship which had sunk off the west coast of Africa, leaving a few survivors to float for days on a raft, driven to starvation, madness and cannibalism. Géricault approached this modern news story like a great historical theme, painting it on a very large canvas in sombre colours, with a dramatic, pyramid-shaped group of figures. The new interests of Romanticism were also shown in Géricault's portraits of patients in a mental asylum and in his melancholy lithographs of the streets of London, inspired by a trip to England in 1821.

Romantic themes were also provided by British writers including William Shakespeare,

Left Théodore Géricault's dramatic painting, *Raft of the Medusa.* (Musée d'Orsay, Paris.)

Above *Massacre at Chios,* a tragic episode recorded by Eugène Delacroix. (Musée du Louvre, Paris.)

Above *The Cross in the Mountains* by Caspar David Friedrich, was commissioned as an altarpiece for a private chapel. (Staatliche Kunstsammlungen, Dresden.)

Lord Byron and Walter Scott. The *Death of Sardanapalus* by Eugène Delacroix (1798-1863) was a violent scene taken from a poem by Byron, of a cruel ruler who ordered all his slaves, mistresses and horses to be put to death.

In Germany, Romanticism had begun to affect literature in the late eighteenth century. The works of writers like Goethe and Schiller stressed the importance of feeling, emotion, and romantic love, and looked to the historical past and to nature for inspiration and spiritual comfort. In the nineteenth century, German painters took up these themes, using landscape to convey spiritual feeling. The paintings of Philip Otto Runge (1777-1810) combine mystical feeling and religious symbolism with accurate scientific observation. He worked on a series of paintings called *The Times of Day*

which he intended to be hung in a specially designed chapel, where specially composed music would be played.

Caspar David Friedrich (1774-1840) believed 'a painter should paint not only what he sees before him but also what he sees within himself.' His landscapes were usually lonely, remote places, in the mountains or along the Baltic seashore, in the twilight of sunrise or sunset, or by moonlight. Solitary figures added to the mood of melancholy and loneliness. Friedrich's landscapes were full of symbolism: he used rocks to represent Christianity and winding paths to show the 'path of life'. A sense of stillness, created by the sombre lighting and his precise brushwork, heightened the religious feeling in Friedrich's landscapes.

While some artists looked to nature to provide spiritual comfort or inspiration, others looked to the historical past. 'The Nazarenes', a group of young German painters working in Italy in the early years of the nineteenth century, aimed to revive the art of the Middle Ages, which they felt was true and direct in style and feeling. They founded a group called 'the Brotherhood of St. Luke', based on a medieval painters' guild, and lived as artist-monks in an abandoned monastery in Rome, growing their hair long, wearing medieval-style clothes and painting, praying and singing together. The leaders, Franz Pforr (1788-1812) and Friedrich Overbeck (1789-1869) had met in 1808 when they were art students in Vienna. They rebelled against their academic training, which was based on Classical Greek and Roman and High Renaissance art, and began to study fifteenth century painters including Dürer and Perugino as well as the early works of Raphael. They copied the methods and styles of these artists,

Left *Italia and Germania* by Friedrich Overbeck. The two women represent Italy and Germany. The Nazarene artists wanted to bring together the best of Italian and Northern European traditions of art. (Gemäldegalerie Neue Meister, Dresden.)

Above *The Wise and Foolish Virgins* by Peter von Cornelius is based on the parable of the Ten Virgins in the New Testament of the Bible. (Gemälde, Düsseldorf.)

sometimes working in the medium of tempera (colours mixed with egg yolk) rather than oils, and learning the technique of fresco. They chose historical subjects, like Pforr's *Entry of the Emperor Rudolf into Basel, 1273*, which he painted in clear, bright colours and with careful, detailed brushwork.

Although Pforr died when only twenty-four, other artists joined the group and carried on its ideas. Peter von Cornelius (1783-1867) aimed to revive the art of fresco, and painted several large wall paintings in churches and other public buildings in Munich.

Like other breakaway groups in the nineteenth century (see the Pre-Raphaelites, Chapter 5) the Nazarenes wanted to revive art by returning to the style and methods of the Middle Ages. Their fascination with medieval life and art is one of the constant themes of Romantic Art.

3 ENGLISH LANDSCAPE PAINTING

In the nineteenth century, people began to take much more interest in landscape painting and this form of art became more highly valued by art critics. Previously, 'view painting' had been considered a humble form of art, much less important than paintings of Biblical, Classical or historical themes. A new interest in landscape developed in England in the eighteenth century, with the fashion for visiting picturesque places, and with the creation of landscaped parks and gardens by the landscape artist Lancelot 'Capability' Brown (1716-83) and his followers. Romantic writers such as the English Lake poets William Wordsworth and Samuel Taylor Coleridge and the French philosopher Jean Jacques Rousseau encouraged the 'back to nature' movement. They showed how the countryside could offer escape and peace in the modern industrial world.

Left *Flatford Mill* by John Constable. This painting is typical of Constable's large oil landscapes. It shows a tranquil summer scene beside the River Stour in Suffolk. (Tate Gallery, London.)

Above Constable's *Branch Hill Pond, Hampstead*. The artist painted many light oil sketches like this one, as well as huge 'finished' works such as *Flatford Mill* opposite. (Victoria and Albert Museum, London).

Some English artists followed the Dutch landscape masters of the seventeenth century in painting their own local countryside. John Constable (1776-1837) painted landscapes of the Stour River valley in Suffolk where he was born. His paintings were usually set in spring or high summer, with the trees in full leaf, and showed simple scenes like a horse being ferried across the river, or a man opening the lock gates. Even after he had moved to London, Constable went on painting the Suffolk landscape which he loved so much. He once wrote 'The sound of water escaping from mill dams, etc., willows, old rotten planks, slimy posts and brickwork – I love such things. Painting with me is but another word for feeling.'

Constable believed artists should work directly from nature, and he made lots of sketches in pencil, watercolour and oil, which he used to compose his large landscapes in the studio. He made a special study of clouds and weather, believing that the sky was the most important element in a landscape. He was always trying new methods of capturing the freshness and 'bloom' of nature – the effect of sunlight after rain, or wind in the leaves or on water. But his experiments – such as scattered highlights of white – were often attacked by the critics, and his landscapes were repeatedly rejected by the Royal Academy for being too humble in their subject matter or 'too green'.

While Constable concentrated on local scenery, his rival at the Royal Academy, Joseph Mallord William Turner (1775-1851) looked more widely for inspiration: to Italy, to the Bible and literature, and to the seventeenth-century

The Norwich School
In choosing to paint local scenery, John Constable was following the example of seventeenth-century Dutch Landscape artists such as Jacob van Ruisdael and Meindert Hobbema. Other nineteenth-century painters also painted local scenery, grouping into regional schools and concentrating on one area of countryside. They include the Barbizon painters in France (see pages 33 and 34) and the Norwich School in England. The artists of the Norwich School (in Norfolk), led by John Crome (1768-1821) and John Sell Cotman (1782-1842) held exhibitions of their paintings at a house in Norwich, between 1805-25. They painted the wide, flat landscape and open skies of Norfolk in fresh oils and watercolours.

Left *Heaving Coals by Moonlight* by J. M. W. Turner. Here Turner has painted the shapes of ship's hulls and rigging dissolving in silvery moonlight. (National Gallery of Art, Washington D.C.)

Above *Landscape Scene in Norfolk* by John Crome. Crome's picturesque scenery and sombre, warm colouring shows the influence of seventeenth-century Dutch artists. (Bury Art Gallery and Museum.)

masters of French Classical landscape painting, Claude Lorraine and Nicolas Poussin. Turner began his career painting watercolour views of buildings and places, but he soon became interested in recording changing effects of atmosphere, light and weather. He sketched landscapes in oil and watercolour, using his sketches and memory to compose large, finished works in the studio. The *Snowstorm: Hannibal crossing the Alps* took a story from Classical history combined with Turner's experience of a violent storm in Yorkshire. Some of his landscapes, although painted from the English countryside, were composed in the manner of Claude and Poussin. Turner wanted landscape art to be more highly regarded, and he worked on a series of landscapes for engraving in a book he called the *Liber Studiorum* (Book of Studies). He had favourite

Samuel Palmer

In the nineteenth century, landscape art was used by painters to convey mood and feelings. This was particularly so with the works of Samuel Palmer (1805-81). Palmer was born in London and began showing his landscape drawings at the Royal Academy at the age of fourteen. He settled in the village of Shoreham in Kent where he joined a group of artists who called themselves 'The Ancients'. They included John Linnell (1792-1882), Edward Calvert (1799-1883) and George Richmond (1809-96). Like the Nazarenes (see pages 14 and 15), The Ancients lived simple lives, concentrating on their art. Palmer painted small, jewel-like landscapes in watercolour or sepia ink, and his works have an intense, spiritual feeling. Throughout his life he was greatly influenced by the visionary artist-poet William Blake (see page 38). With *In a Shoreham Garden* (above), Palmer conveys the exuberance of nature. (Victoria and Albert Museum, London.)

The *Burning of the Houses of Parliament*. Turner recorded this dramatic episode in 1834. The fire provided him with an exciting subject, with flames and smoke reflected in the River Thames. (Philadelphia Museum of Art.)

themes he returned to time and again: the sea, dramatic storms, sunrise and sunset.

In 1819, Turner made the first of several visits to Italy, where the brilliant light and sunshine inspired him to experiment with new ways of representing light and atmosphere. His compositions, too, became freer and more abstract, sometimes based around a swirling, circular shape. He loved effects of steam, smoke or mist, dissolving form into pure colour, as in the *Burning of the Houses of Parliament* or *Rain Steam Speed: The Great Western Railway*. Critics thought his later works looked strange, with their shimmering veils of colour, and called them 'pictures of nothing, and very like'. They were amazed that

Turner often completed his pictures as they hung on the walls of the Royal Academy just before an exhibition opened. In his exhibition works and in his spontaneous sketches which he called 'colour beginnings', Turner brought a new approach to landscape art.

Thomas Girtin
Another English painter, Thomas Girtin (1775-1802), worked closely with Turner in the mid-1790s. Girtin painted in watercolours and was the first artist to realize the possibilities of this medium. He was only twenty-seven when he died, but during his short life he revolutionized landscape painting in watercolours, at which he excelled.

4 ART IN NORTH AMERICA

Home in the Woods by Thomas Cole. In this painting Cole depicts the struggle of early American settlers to survive in a wild, untamed countryside. (Reynolds Museum, Winston Salem, N. Carolina.)

In the early nineteenth century, much of the American continent was still wild, unspoiled country. But there was already awareness that this natural paradise could be threatened by advancing civilization. As the artist Thomas Cole wrote, 'The painter of American scenery has, indeed, privileges superior to any other; all nature here is new to art.'

Cole (1801-48) was the first American painter to concentrate on painting landscape. He travelled from New York along the Hudson river valley in search of scenery, founding the first school of American painting, the Hudson River School. Cole's landscapes are often breathtaking panoramas, with human figures dwarfed by wild countryside stretching away to a wide horizon. He also painted landscapes with historical or allegorical themes, such as the decline and fall of civilizations, or 'the voyage of life'.

Asher B. Durand (1796-1886), another painter in the Hudson River School, liked to paint out of doors. His views of the Hudson valley showed careful detail which reflected his training as an engraver. Cole's pupil, Frederick Church (1826-1900) travelled further afield, to South America, the Alps and the Arctic, in search of awe-inspiring scenery of mountains, jungles and rocky deserts, (see picture on page 5). His subjects included the Niagara Falls, the icebergs of the Arctic and the volcanic mountain of Cotopaxi in Ecuador.

Sunset Going Down Over the Sea by the Luminist painter John Frederick Kensett. The painter has concentrated entirely on the light of sunset, reducing his composition to sea and sky only. (Metropolitan Museum of Art, New York.)

By the middle of the century, painters including John Frederick Kensett (1816-72), Fitz Hugh Lane (1804-65) and Martin Johnson Heade (1819-1904) were showing increasing interest in capturing effects of light and atmosphere. These effects have come to be known as luminism, a word used to describe landscapes painted in a brilliant midday light, with every detail in telescopic focus and an almost magical stillness. In a luminist landscape, there is an overwhelming sense of light, space and air.

Folk or primitive art became very popular in America in the nineteenth century. Folk artists usually had no professional training and often worked anonymously, selling their paintings as they travelled from place to place. Portraits, landscapes and pictures of farm and wild animals were all popular subjects.

The best known of the American 'primitive' artists of the early nineteenth century is Edward Hicks (1780-1849) who began his career as a coach and sign painter. He was a Quaker and he painted many pictures with Biblical themes. There are over a hundred versions of his *Peaceable Kingdom* which takes its theme from a Bible story about people and animals all living in harmony together.

Fur Trappers Descending the Missouri by George Caleb Bingham. Bingham's painting captures the stillness and tranquillity of the river. (Metropolitan Museum of Art, New York.)

American wildlife

Some of the exotic plant and animal life of the American countryside was captured in the beautiful watercolours of John James Audubon (1785-1851). Audubon was born in the West Indies and brought up in France, where he became interested in drawing birds and other subjects from nature. He settled in North America in 1803, painting portraits and teaching drawing to earn a living. He followed his special interests of hunting, painting wildlife and taxidermy (the process of stuffing animal skins) in his spare time. By the 1820s, he was working on his masterpiece, the illustrations for *Birds of America,* which recorded almost five hundred native species in watercolour drawings. (See his *Ivory-billed Woodpecker* above)

Genre painting (about everyday life and activities), inspired by the wild and sometimes dangerous lives of the European pioneers and the native Americans, became popular in America in the early nineteenth century. Paintings by artists like George Caleb Bingham (1811-79) and George Catlin (1796-1872) captured the sense of adventure in a land where nature was still untamed. Bingham painted in the frontier areas of Missouri and the Mid West, recording the lives of boatmen, fur trappers and settlers along the Missouri River. There is a haunting silence and stillness about his river scenes which are full of light, air and reflections. William Sidney Mount

The Gross Clinic by Thomas Eakins. With this subject Eakins was following a tradition which included artists like the great seventeenth-century Dutch painter Rembrandt. (Jefferson College, Philadelphia.)

The Blue Boat by Winslow Homer. Homer painted this watercolour in a crisp, fresh style which shows the influence of Japanese prints. (Private collection.)

(1807-68) painted life on Long Island, where he was born. He followed the Dutch genre painters of the seventeenth century, choosing scenes of work and leisure in domestic or rural settings – cider-making, bargaining for a horse, mending tools or dancing. George Catlin and Seth Eastman (1805-75) recorded with accuracy and detail the lives and customs of the native Americans, who were fast disappearing with the advance of the white settlers.

Winslow Homer (1836-1910) trained as a lithographer and began his career engraving scenes from the Civil War (1861-65) for the magazine *Harper's Weekly*. His later genre paintings ranged from simple domestic or rural scenes, such as berry picking in the autumn, or a country classroom, to life in the fashionable seaside resorts. With his careful observation of light and weather, and his fresh, unsentimental approach, Homer brought a new realism to American genre painting.

Thomas Eakins (1844-1916) trained in Paris in the 1860s, where he saw the work of the Realist painter Gustave Courbet (see pages 32-3) and studied earlier artists including the seventeenth-century Spanish artist Diego Velázquez. Back in America, Eakins developed his own Realist style, making careful, scientific studies of perspective, anatomy and light, and using the new art of photography to help him understand form and movement. He even dissected corpses, while researching *The Gross Clinic*, which showed a surgeon working on a dissection in front of his students. The painting shocked the public and the art critics with its realistic treatment of the subject.

5 THE PRE-RAPHAELITES

When first shown, John Millais's *Christ in the House of His Parents*, was criticized for showing the holy family in a humble, realistic setting. (Tate Gallery, London.)

In 1848, a number of paintings were shown at the Royal Academy in London, signed with the secret initials P.R.B. The Pre-Raphaelite Brotherhood was a group of young artists, all aged about twenty. They were rebelling against the style of art which was being taught at the Royal Academy and at other art schools, which they considered to be artificial in subject and style, and dark and muddy in colour. They looked back to artists of the fifteenth century – before the time of the Renaissance master Raphael – who inspired them with their serious subjects, careful, detailed brushwork and bright, fresh colours.

The Pre-Raphaelites were led by John Everett Millais (1829-96), William Holman Hunt (1827-1910), and Dante Gabriel Rossetti (1828-82). They talked together and wrote down their

ideas on art, and made a list of all the artists and other famous people they admired. They chose subjects from the Bible or from poetry and legend, using sources from Shakespeare, the poets Keats and Tennyson, and the legend of King Arthur. They tried to paint their subjects as truthfully and accurately as possible, making careful studies of every detail, from medieval swords and spears to wild flowers and foliage. They used bright colours, painting on to a wet white background so that their paintings looked much lighter and fresher than others of the time, which were usually painted on a brown background.

Rossetti's painting of the Annunciation of the Virgin Mary *Ecce Ancilla Domini* (see page 27), was painted in bright, primary colours with lots of white. Millais's *Christ in the House of His*

Above Millais' *Ophelia*. Rossetti's wife, Elizabeth Siddal, posed for this painting of the tragic drowning scene from Shakespeare's *Hamlet*. (Tate Gallery, London.)

Parents shocked the critics and the public because it showed Jesus as an ordinary little boy with his family in a real, humble carpenter's shop. The novelist Charles Dickens attacked it as 'mean, repulsive and revolting,' but the influential critic John Ruskin came to the Pre-Raphaelites' defence.

The Pre-Raphaelites believed that art should have a serious, moral purpose. As well as subjects from the Bible they painted social themes, such as William Holman Hunt's *The Awakening Conscience* (see cover), which showed an unmarried woman realizing that she must give up her relationship with her lover. Set in a typical English Victorian sitting room, the picture is full of symbolism, like the cat playing with a bird under the table and the print of the Biblical story of the woman who committed adultery, above the piano.

Scenes from literature were also popular. For Millais's *Ophelia*, a tragic scene from Shakespeare's *Hamlet*, the favourite Pre-Raphaelite model Elizabeth Siddal posed in a bath kept warm by lamps placed underneath.

Above *The Last of England* by Ford Madox Brown. This painting was inspired by the often sad departure of emigrants to the far-off shores of Australia. (Birmingham City Art Gallery.)

Left In his painting of the 'Annunciation', *Ecce Ancilla Domini*, Dante Gabriel Rossetti has tried to portray a simple vision of the Virgin Mary, using lots of white to convey purity. (Tate Gallery, London.)

The background was painted from nature by Millais on the banks of the River Ewell in Surrey. Dante Gabriel Rossetti's favourite writer was the Italian medieval poet Dante, and he made many small, jewel-like oil and watercolour paintings illustrating scenes from Dante's life and poetry.

The Pre-Raphaelite Brotherhood lasted less than ten years as a group, but other artists took up the Pre-Raphaelite style and subjects of painting. Ford Madox Brown (1821-93) painted *Work* in 1865, showing a street scene near the artist's home in Hampstead, London. The painting depicted all the different social classes which made up Victorian society, from street beggars to the leisured upper classes. Even the dogs in the picture represented different social classes!

Brown's best known painting, *The Last of England*, showed emigrants on board ship, leaving for Australia. He also painted landscapes in the Pre-Raphaelite style, as did William Holman Hunt and another, very popular artist William Dyce (1806-64).

6 SCULPTURE IN THE NINETEENTH CENTURY

The Three Graces, by Antonio Canova. The sculptor has borrowed Classical ideals to create a Neoclassical sculpture, with beautiful flowing forms carved from smooth white Carrara marble. (Belvoir Castle, Leicestershire.)

Sculpture was a popular form of art during the nineteenth century. Bronze or stone statues, commemorating heroes or important events, were set up in public streets and squares, and today we can still see nineteenth century sculpture all around us, in city centres, parks, churches and graveyards. Sculpture was also widely used to decorate the inside and outside of town halls, opera houses, theatres, hotels and private houses.

Like painters of the time, sculptors worked in a variety of styles, but Neoclassicism, inspired by the Classical statues of Greece and Rome, was the dominant style. The outstanding Neoclassical sculptors of the early nineteenth century were the Italian Antonio Canova (1757-1822) and the Dane Bertel Thorvaldsen (1770-1844) who settled in Rome in 1797. Both men carved calm, idealized statues in smooth white Carrara marble, representing Classical subjects or portraits of patrons in the Neoclassical style, like Thorvaldsen's portrait bust of the banker Thomas Hope, or Canova's portrait of Pauline Borghese as a reclining Venus. One of the most popular statues of the century was the Neoclassical nude *Greek Slave*, by the American sculptor Hiram Powers

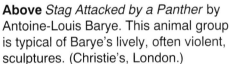

Above *Stag Attacked by a Panther* by
Antoine-Louis Barye. This animal group
is typical of Barye's lively, often violent,
sculptures. (Christie's, London.)

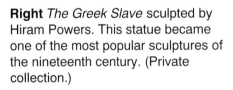

Right *The Greek Slave* sculpted by
Hiram Powers. This statue became
one of the most popular sculptures of
the nineteenth century. (Private
collection.)

(1805-73) which was taken on tour in the
United States in 1847 and was a great success
when shown at the Great Exhibition in London
in 1851. Replicas of the statue were sold to
private collectors in Europe and the United
States.

Romanticism did not have the same impact on
sculpture as it had on painting. But it was
reflected in the emotion and energy of works
like *Departure of the Volunteers* by François
Rude (1784-1855), carved on the Arc de
Triomphe in Paris, and inspired the crowded
sculptures of Auguste Préault (1809-79).

Antoine-Louis Barye (1796-1875) specialized in
dramatic, often violent animal groups and
figures. He had begun his career working for a
goldsmith, making small animal figures for
jewellery, then in 1831 he cast his first large
scale bronze of a tiger. Barye worked from
sketches of wild animals in the Paris Zoo,
bringing his sculptures to life by their lively
modelling and the flickering play of light over
their surfaces.

The most celebrated sculptor of the nineteenth
century was Auguste Rodin (1840-1917). He
was born in Paris, and studied drawing with

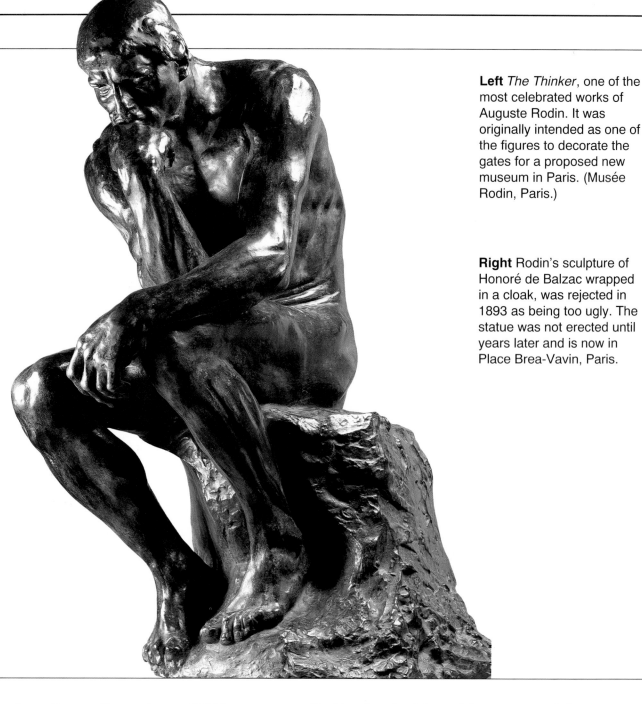

Left *The Thinker*, one of the most celebrated works of Auguste Rodin. It was originally intended as one of the figures to decorate the gates for a proposed new museum in Paris. (Musée Rodin, Paris.)

Right Rodin's sculpture of Honoré de Balzac wrapped in a cloak, was rejected in 1893 as being too ugly. The statue was not erected until years later and is now in Place Brea-Vavin, Paris.

the sculptor Barye. From about 1864 he worked as a mason, carving decorative figures for the Stock Exchange building in Brussels. In 1875 he visited Italy, where he studied Classical and Renaissance sculpture, including the works of Michelangelo. Two years later, Rodin exhibited his first lifesize statue, *The Age of Bronze*, which was so lifelike that the artist was accused of making a plaster cast directly from the model! The figures which followed, the *Walking Man* and the study for *St John the Baptist Preaching*, showed the same lifelike quality.

Rodin sketched from life using models moving around his studio, before modelling his works in wax or clay. Casts might then be made from bronze, or marble carved following the wax or clay model. Rodin wanted to make sculptures which would be touched as well as seen, and he used expressive poses and broken, textured surfaces to create interest and convey emotion or energy. Some critics thought his works often looked sketchy or unfinished, rather like Impressionist paintings (see page 35), but for Rodin even part of a figure could be a complete sculpture.

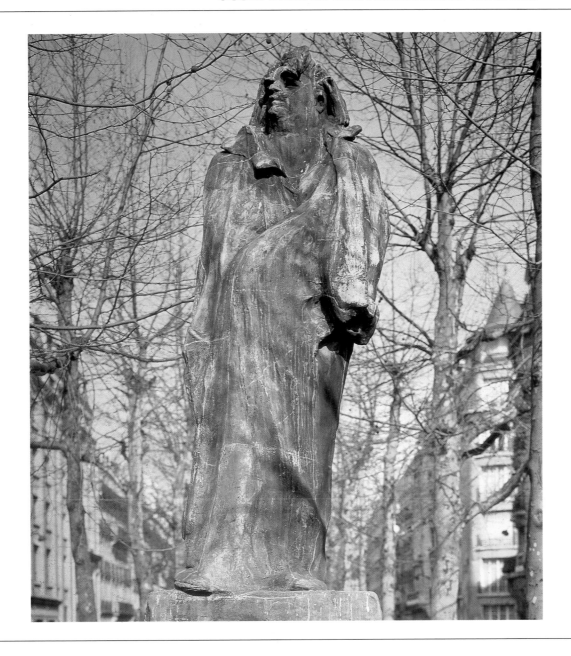

In 1879, Rodin was commissioned to make the gates for a new museum of decorative arts in Paris. Rodin's gates, called the *Gates of Hell* were inspired by Ghiberti's *Gates of Paradise*, made for the Baptistery of Florence Cathedral in the fifteenth century. Ghiberti had worked in regular bronze panels, but Rodin's design was much freer, allowing his figures to twist and flow. In the end, the museum was never completed and nor were the gates, but the commission did give Rodin ideas for over two hundred sculptures including *The Thinker* (above left) and *The Kiss*.

Although Rodin became very famous, some of his works were strongly criticized. His portrait of the novelist Honoré de Balzac (above), showing the writer wrapped in a cloak which hides his body, was attacked as formless and ugly, and rejected by the people who commissioned it. Today, Balzac is one of Rodin's most famous portraits of nineteenth-century celebrities, which included the writers Baudelaire and Bernard Shaw, the composer Gustav Mahler and the dancer Nijinsky. After his death in 1917, the sculptor's last studio in Paris was opened as the Rodin Museum.

7 REALISM IN FRANCE

The Stone Breakers by Gustave Courbet. He was an ardent socialist, whose paintings, showing everyday lives of hardship and poverty, conveyed a social message. (Staatliche Kunstsammlungen, Dresden.)

By the middle of the nineteenth century, there was growing awareness of the social and economic problems caused by the Industrial Revolution. There was widespread unemployment and poverty in the cities, and those who were lucky enough to have jobs often suffered long hours and poor working conditions. The concern of some artists and writers about these problems was reflected in their works, which showed the lives of ordinary people at work and at home. These artists were known as Realists.

Realist art often shocked both critics and the public because it broke the rules taught by the art schools. Realist artists began painting humble, everyday subjects on a scale previously used only for grand Biblical,

historical or Classical subjects. They also experimented with new ways of handling paint, using broad brush strokes and thicker paint, so that the picture itself had texture and interest. Some artists used photographs to help them understand form and movement, or to compose their pictures.

In France, the leading Realist painter was Gustave Courbet (1819-77). He painted simple, everyday subjects like the country funeral *Burial at Ornans* or *The Stone Breakers* (above), showing two men hard at work, breaking stones by a roadside. He used thick paint, handled with a broad brush or a palette knife, and drab, earthy colours. He said that 'Painting is an essentially concrete art and can only consist of the presentation of real and existing

Above *The Water Gate*, a peaceful riverside scene by Charles François Daubigny. He was one of the Barbizon painters, a group of artists who encouraged the practice of painting out of doors. (Musée d'Orsay, Paris.)

Right *Fields with Trees and Cottages* by Jean-Baptiste Camille Corot. He produced a huge number of works and his later paintings have a dream-like quality, with misty colouring and flickering light. (Christie's, London.)

things. I cannot paint an angel because I have never seen one.' When Courbet painted nudes they were real people, not idealized figures, and when he painted landscapes or seascapes they were of real places. (See also page 8.)

After his paintings were criticized for being vulgar and rejected by the International Exhibition in Paris in 1855, Courbet set up his own Realist exhibition. In his life, as well as in his art, he was a rebel. He was imprisoned for a while, then forced into exile in Switzerland after taking part in riots supporting the Paris Commune of 1871. This was a committee set up in opposition to the French government, and during that time crowds took to the streets to demonstrate the power of the ordinary people against the French National Assembly.

Realism dealt with modern, everyday subjects, showing the lives of ordinary people, but it also changed the way artists looked at the landscape. In France, the influence of the English Landscape School began to be felt from the 1820s, with an exhibition of Constable's paintings in Paris, and the works of English artists living in France, such as Richard Parkes Bonington (1802-28). These artists encouraged sketching from nature, out of doors. Georges Michel (1763-1843) painted the fields and heaths around Paris with bold, free brushwork and dark earthy colours. Like Michel, Jean-Baptiste Camille Corot (1796-1875) began sketching landscapes in oil in the open air, but the brilliant light of Italy, which he visited in 1824, encouraged him to mix white with all his colours, giving them a fresh, light quality.

The Gleaners by Jean-François Millet. This picture of poor women gathering scraps of corn after the harvest became one of the best-known paintings of the nineteenth century. (Musée d'Orsay.)

In the 1830s, a group of landscape artists settled around the village of Barbizon in the Forest of Fontainebleau near Paris. The Barbizon painters included Théodore Rousseau (1812-67) and Charles François Daubigny (1817-78). They wanted to leave city life behind and paint directly from nature in the open air. Rousseau was especially interested in effects of weather and light at different times of day. Daubigny painted peaceful river scenes from his studio boat on the rivers Seine and Oise. In their desire to paint in the open air and to capture subtle changes in light and weather, the Barbizon School anticipated the work of the Impressionists (see opposite page).

Jean-François Millet (1814-75) knew and worked alongside the painters at Barbizon, where he settled in 1849, living in great poverty. Millet concentrated on painting simple rural landscapes, showing peasants working in the fields. Paintings like *The Sower,* and *The Gleaners* (above), have a haunting quality with their flat, melancholy landscape, drab colours and isolated figures.

Impressionism

The Impressionists were the most important breakaway group of artists to emerge during the nineteenth century. They included Claude Monet (1840-1926), Pierre Auguste Renoir (1841-1919), Camille Pissarro (1830-1903) and Alfred Sisley (1839-99). They rejected Classical and historical themes and chose modern subjects like people boating on the River Seine or relaxing in Parisian cafés or parks, or at the theatre or ballet. They wanted to capture the immediate visual impression of what they saw under changing conditions of light and weather. They painted landscapes in the open air, working in bright sunlight and they experimented with techniques, using short strokes or dots of colour and avoiding dark outlines and traditional ways of painting light and shade. Critics thought their paintings looked sketchy and unfinished and their works were rejected by the official Paris Salon. From 1874, the Impressionists held their own exhibitions in Paris, becoming the most important and influential art movement in the second half of the nineteenth century. The Impressionists and the Post-Impressionists who followed them, including such famous nineteenth-century artists as Paul Cézanne (1839-1906) and Vincent van Gogh (1853-90), are discussed separately in *Impressionism*, another book in this series. Above is a view of Paris, *Place de Havre*, by Camille Pissarro (Chicago Art Institute, U.S.A.).

8 JAPANESE ART

The Carpenter's Yard by Katushika Hokusai, one of the celebrated *Ukiyo-e* artists of nineteenth-century Japan. This is one of his 'Thirty-six Views of Mount Fuji'. (British Museum, London.)

Japanese artists had become skilled at colour printing from woodblocks during the eighteenth century: up to thirty blocks (one for each colour) were sometimes used to print a single design. The *Ukiyo-e* or 'Floating World' school specialized in scenes of everyday life, at home or in town, and portraits of actors and actresses. These decorative prints were pasted to walls or screens in the home, and used to illustrate books and greetings cards. Landscapes, and bird and flower prints were also popular.

European artists first saw Japanese prints in the nineteenth century, when some arrived in Paris as packing for china. Artists, including the Impressionists, were impressed by the Japanese printmakers' strong sense of design and pattern, unusual compositions and bold, flat areas of colour.

The decorative appeal and inventiveness of Japanese prints is illustrated by the *Thirty-six Views of Mount Fuji* by Katsushika Hokusai (1760-1849). Hokusai had begun making

The Revenge of Igagoe by Uragawa Kuniyoshi, another *Ukiyo-e* artist. Kuniyoshi often illustrated the Samurai warriors of Japanese history. In this print he has shown a warrior engaged in fighting off his foes in a style rather similar to one used in modern western cartoon comics.

theatrical prints in the *Ukiyo-e* style but soon became more interested in landscape. As well as his series focusing on the dramatic, cone-shaped mountain near Tokyo, he printed series of *Waterfalls*, *Bridges* and *Flowers*. His strong, stylized designs and brilliant colours were admired by Edouard Manet and the Impressionists.

Ando Hiroshige (1797-1858) trained in the *Ukiyo-e* school, but from the 1830s he concentrated on bird and flower themes and landscapes. He is most admired for his sensitive treatment of light, weather and atmosphere, in landscapes in mist, rain or snow.

Uragawa Kuniyoshi (1798-1861) took his subjects from Japanese history and legend. His large, often humorous colour prints, sometimes showing samurai warriors engaged in violent battles with monsters, are as bold and melodramatic in style as the illustrations in western comic magazines.

9 PRINTMAKING AND PHOTOGRAPHY

The English artist and poet William Blake (1757-1827) made this print to illustrate his 'Book of Job'. The print was produced from a coloured engraving.

During the nineteenth century, wood engraving, a method of printmaking which used blocks of hard wood, allowed faster and cheaper reproduction for book and magazine illustration and copies of popular paintings. Wood engraving involved the use of very hard wooden blocks for printing. The wood was cut across the grain (from sections across the trunk of a tree) rather than parallel to the tree (along the trunk) as in the older art of woodcut. Wood engraving allowed clean fine lines to be cut into the block, which show as white in the

print as ink was only rolled on to the remaining uncut section.

Woodcut had been widely used in the fifteenth century. It enjoyed a revival from the 1830s with the increasing interest in medieval art. Later in the century it was used by Arts and Crafts artists to illustrate books of legend, poetry and history (see pages 42, 43 and 44).

Lithography, a new method of surface printing from stone, was invented at the end of the

Above Honoré Daumier's cartoons poked fun at the pretensions of middle class life. The lithograph shows a couple in front of their portrait at the Paris salon.

Right *The Guardian Angel*, a photograph taken in 1868 by the English photographer, Julia Margaret Cameron (1815-79). She created haunting images, often with religious or literary themes.

eighteenth century. The artist's design was drawn on the special lithographic stone in greasy crayon or ink and fixed with chemicals. The stone surface was then wetted with water and rolled with greasy ink which stuck only to the greasy parts of the design. The stone was then passed through a press to transfer the inked design on to paper.

As well as being cheap, lithography could be used for both simple linear designs and colour prints, and could make huge numbers of copies. Various effects, with opaque or delicate textured washes, could be achieved. In France, it became the popular medium for magazine cartoons and caricatures, such as those by the political and social satirist Honoré Daumier (1810-79).

By the end of the century, colour lithography was being used for a new art form: the poster. The French artist Henri de Toulouse Lautrec (1864-1901) began designing posters in 1891. His subjects were dancers and circus clowns,

Woman Washing, a print by the American artist Mary Cassatt (see page 43). Her work was greatly influenced by the art of Japanese woodblock printers, whose work she saw in Paris.

scenes from music halls, theatres, café bars and Paris night clubs, like the Moulin Rouge cabaret. Lautrec was inspired by Japanese woodblock prints, choosing unusual viewpoints, flattening space and using bold colours and semi-abstract shapes to design lively, colourful images.

The technique which was to have the greatest impact on nineteenth century art was photography. The amateur inventor Joseph Niépce had discovered how to fix negatives on to a metal plate using bitumen in the 1820s. Another Frenchman, Louis Daguerre, was using a silvered copper plate to make 'daguerrotype' prints by the 1830s. The first true photographs – negatives from which any number of prints could be taken – were made by the English scientist Henry Fox Talbot around 1840. He discovered how to make negatives by soaking paper in silver chloride to make it light sensitive, then exposing it to light through a lens.

Modern poster art began with the lively colour lithographs of Henri de Toulouse Lautrec. He was a superb draughtsman, with a wonderful gift for conveying movement and atmosphere with a few simple strokes.

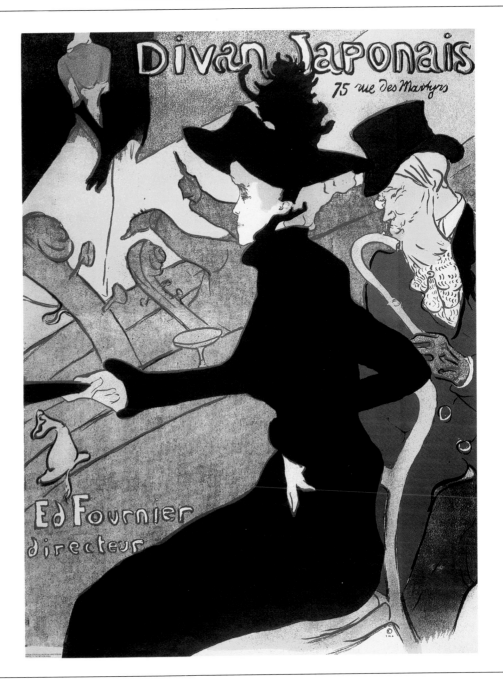

Mezzotint was a popular method for reproducing artists' works. The engraver roughened a copper or steel plate with a tool to produce an overall textured surface (or 'burr'), which could catch the ink and print velvety black. Designs and lighter areas could then be produced by reducing or removing the textured 'burr' by scraping or polishing the surface of the plate. Mezzotints spread the fame of artists by allowing people to buy cheap printed copies of their works.

Aquatint, a method of etching in tone, was especially suitable for reproducing the soft and transparent effects of watercolours and wash drawings. Powdered resin was shaken on to a copper plate and fixed on to it by heating. Some areas were then removed to print darker while others were blocked out with varnish to print lighter, and then the plate was dipped in acid, which produced a pitted or textured surface, producing the grainy effect of watercolour when printed.

10 THE LATER CENTURY

Right 'Woodpecker' tapestry, designed by William Morris *c.* 1885. (William Morris Gallery, London.)

Far right *Isolde*, a magazine illustration by the English artist Aubrey Beardsley (1872-98). His stylized drawings are typical of the Art Nouveau style of the 1890s. (Private collection.)

ISOLDE

The invention of labour-saving machines and mass-production of goods and materials in factories and workshops altered people's lifestyles as well as the clothes, furniture and household goods they owned. Although machines generally improved the quality of people's lives, they also led to a decline in standards of manufacture which by the end of the century was becoming increasingly apparent. In England, a growing awareness of the need to preserve qualities of design and craftsmanship inspired the founding of the Arts and Crafts movement, led by the artist-designer William Morris (1834-96) and the influential art critic John Ruskin (1819-1900).

The Arts and Crafts movement rejected the shoddy standards of mass production and the fussy and over-elaborate designs which had become popular. Arts and Crafts designers took inspiration from the art of the Middle Ages, establishing an 'Art-workers Guild' which was based on medieval artists' guilds, and drawing on Gothic motifs and style.

In 1861, Morris founded the firm of Morris, Marshall Faulkner & Co, with workshops producing hand-made furniture, stained glass, carpets, tapestries, wallpapers and fabrics to designs by Morris and artists including Dante Gabriel Rossetti and Edward Burne Jones

Women artists in the nineteenth century

In nineteenth century Europe and America, sketching and watercolour painting were popular pastimes for women of the middle and upper classes. Working as a professional artist however, was not generally considered a suitable occupation although some did succeed in exhibiting and selling their work. In England, Helen Allingham (1849-1926) painted charming cottage and garden scenes in watercolours with painstaking detail, and Kate Greenaway (1846-1901) used watercolours for her delicate illustrations for children's books. In France, Rosa Bonheur (1822-99) specialized in painting animals, especially horses, exhibiting regularly at the Paris Salon after 1841. Mary Cassatt (1845-1926) an American working in Paris, and Berthe Morisot (1841-95) were both members of the Impressionist group of artists. Cassatt painted women and children in soft oils or pastels and produced prints strongly influenced by the Japanese style (see page 40). Morisot, early on, was influenced by the French painter Corot, but after marrying Edouard Manet's younger brother, she joined the Impressionists. She painted interiors and garden scenes, with fresh, flickering brush strokes. Women also played an important part in the Arts and Crafts movement, as painters, illustrators, potters, metalworkers and embroiderers. *A Waggon and a Team of Horses* (above) is by Rosa Bonheur (Wallace Collection, London.)

(1833-98). Morris's distinctive designs, with their closely-worked decorative patterns became very popular and are still being printed and sold today. When he married, Morris asked his friend, the architect Philip Webb (1831-1915) to design a house for him. The Red House, Bexley Heath, Kent took its inspiration from traditional English manor houses and the Gothic Revival style, and encouraged a new style in architecture.

Exhibitions of Arts and Crafts work and design magazines like *The Studio* spread the influence of this new style: soon every branch of the arts was affected, including book design and illustration, with the founding of Morris's own Kelmscott Press in 1890.

In America, the Arts and Crafts style inspired the setting up of art potteries like the Rookwood Pottery, founded in Cincinnati in

Above An earthenware dish painted with a peacock pattern, designed by William de Morgan (1839-1917). He illustrated pottery and ceramics in designs taken from Turkish and Persian art.

Right A Rookwood Pottery earthenware jar made in the United States about the turn of the century.

1880, which produced decorative vases and jugs with rich green or brown glazes, and the Newcomb College Pottery, established in 1895. In New York, Elbert Hubbard (1856-1915) founded a Guild of Craftsmen, the Roycrofters, based on Morris's ideas, and made oak furniture, metalwork and books. Another furniture designer, Gustav Stickley (1857-1942) designed furniture influenced by the Arts and Crafts pieces he had seen on a visit to Europe.

By the end of the century, new attitudes to painting were emerging, under the influence of photography and the Impressionist movement. Some artists, reacting against story-telling genre pictures and detailed, photographic-type paintings, began to experiment with imaginative subjects and freer brushwork. The American painter James Abbot McNeill Whistler (1834-1903), who settled in London in 1859, believed that painting should affect people in the same way as music. He used free, soft brush strokes, concentrating on tone, colour and pattern rather than line. As a student in Paris, Whistler had studied the works of the Spanish master Velázquez in the

Charles Rennie Mackintosh (1868-1928)

Mackintosh was a Scottish architect and designer prominent in the Arts and Crafts Movement. He achieved great success, particularly in Europe where his elegant designs were greatly admired. His design for the Glasgow School of Art (begun in 1896) is considered to be the first original example of Art Nouveau architecture in Britain, although much of his work, including his graceful furnishings and interior decor, are quite unlike Art Nouveau. This beautifully proportioned room at the School of Art (above) with its tall bow windows and granite fireplace, houses some of Mackintosh's larger pieces of furniture.

Whistler's *Falling Rocket*. This is the painting which triggered a famous libel case between the artist and the critic John Ruskin. (Institute of Arts, Detroit).

Louvre, admiring their cool grey tones and uncluttered sense of form and pattern. He also admired living French painters like Courbet, and was impressed by the Japanese prints then becoming popular in Europe.

In his own works, whether portraits, interiors or scenes on the River Thames, Whistler tended to simplify and flatten space, concentrating on shape and pattern and often using cool colours. He gave many of his paintings musical titles such as Symphony, Arrangement or Nocturne. The *Nocturne in*

Black and Gold: Falling Rocket, painted in 1874, was inspired by a display of fireworks over a London park. Its free, semi-abstract design shocked the critics and led to a famous libel trial in which Whistler sued the art critic John Ruskin for accusing him of 'flinging a pot of paint in the public's face'. During the 1860s, Whistler began signing his works with a butterfly motif, which reflected the decorative charm of his works. (See also picture on page 9.) With their simplified forms and cool, clear tones, Whistler's paintings heralded the art of the coming twentieth century.

GLOSSARY

Abstract art Images based on shapes and forms, not representing anything else.

Allegorical An image or theme used to symbolize something else.

Anatomy The science concerned with the physical structure of animals and plants.

Art Nouveau A style of art and architecture in the 1890s. It was characterized by flowing, coiling outlines and stylized natural forms such as flowers and leaves.

Barbizon School A group of landscape painters based at the village of Barbizon in the Forest of Fontainebleau in France, in the mid-nineteenth century.

Biblical Relating to the Bible.

Bronze A type of metal, made from copper and tin, used for making tools and sculpture.

Ceramics The art of producing objects in clay, porcelain, china etc.

Classical mythology Stories and beliefs relating to Ancient Greece and Rome.

Derby Day The day of the famous annual horse race, held at Epsom Downs in Surrey, England every June.

Engraving A print made from an engraved (cut) hard surface such as metal, wood or stone.

Etching A method of print-making, using acid to burn out a design on to metal or glass.

Form Shape.

Fresco A way of painting directly on to newly-plastered walls. The picture itself is often called a fresco.

Genre Describing a painting of people engaged in everyday activities.

Gothic The style of architecture first used in western Europe from the twelfth to sixteenth centuries.

Gothic Revival A style in the nineteenth century which imitated medieval Gothic.

Hudson River School A group of American artists centred in or near the Hudson River valley in the 1800s.

Impressionism The name given to the art of a group of painters working in the latter half of the nineteenth century, who concentrated on recording the effects of light and colour.

Idealized Represented in an ideal or perfect form rather than naturally.

Industrial Revolution The time during the eighteenth and nineteenth centuries in which European countries and the United States changed from producing mainly agricultural goods to mainly industrial goods.

Interiors Pictures of the inside of rooms or buildings.

Lithography A method of making prints from a special lithographic stone on which a design is made with a greasy crayon or ink and then pressed on to paper.

Media In art, the different materials and methods of production.

Middle Ages The period between the end of the Dark Ages (at the end of the Roman Empire) to the Renaissance, from about the sixth to sixteenth centuries.

Moral Concerned with a sense of right and wrong.

Nazarenes A group of artists working in Germany in the early nineteenth century.

Neoclassical A late eighteenth and early nineteenth-century style of art and architecture based on the imitation of surviving Ancient Greek and Roman models.

Panoramas Wide landscape views in all directions.

Patronage The support given by a person (patron) who sponsors or aids artists.

Perspective The science of showing objects in space on a two-dimensional (flat) surface.

Pre-Raphaelites A group of artists in nineteenth-century England who painted in the detailed style they considered to be typical of medieval and early Renaissance artists.

Realism A style of art that seeks to represent the familiar, everyday aspects of life.

Resin A plant substance used for hardening.

Romanticism A movement in the arts in the late eighteenth and nineteenth centuries, characterized by an emphasis on emotions and feeling.

Royal Academy A society founded in London in 1768 to encourage painting, sculpture and design in England.

Samurai warriors Japanese fighters and aristocrats.

Symbolism The representation of something by something else.

Tempera Painting with pigments (colours) mixed with egg-yolk and water. This was a common painting technique until the late fifteenth century.

Tone The quality of colour.

Visionary A spiritual person, someone who has visions of another life.

Wood cuts Prints made by cutting areas of a block of wood, to form a picture. When the block is covered with ink and pressed on paper, the cut design is printed.

FURTHER READING

Davidson, Rosemary *What is Art?* (Oxford Books, 1993).

Powell, Jillian *Famous Artists* (Wayland, 1993).

Powell, Jillian *Painting and Sculpture* (Wayland, 1989).

Treheuz, Julian *Victorian Painting* (Thames and Hudson, 1993).

For older readers

Gombrich, E. G. *The Story of Art* (Phaidon, reprinted 1989).

Murray, Peter and Linda *Dictionary of Art and Artists* (Penguin, reprinted 1991).

Osborne, Forfar and Chilvers *The Oxford Dictionary of Art* (O.U.P. 1988).

Petersen, K. and Wilson, J. J. *Women Artists* (The Women's Press Ltd., reprinted 1985).

WHERE TO SEE NINETEENTH-CENTURY ART

You can see examples of nineteenth-century art in museums and galleries in most major cities in Europe and America.

In Britain, the National Gallery, the Tate Gallery and the Victoria and Albert Museum all have good collections of art of this period. The Tate Gallery, in particular, has many examples of Pre-Raphaelite art, and a large collection of Turner paintings. Major galleries in Edinburgh, Glasgow and Cardiff also have collections of nineteenth-century art, as do most art galleries in larger towns and cities in the U.K.

The William Morris Museum at Walthamstow in north London has an exhibition of Morris's work and that of other members of the Arts and Crafts movement.

In Paris, the Musée du Louvre and Musée d'Orsay have many examples of Neo-classical, Romantic and Realist paintings, and works by the German Romantic artists can be found in galleries in major German cities.

Most American art of the period is to be found in museums and galleries in the United States.

INDEX

Numbers in **bold** refer to illustrations